Callisto 5

A play

Alan Ayckbourn

Samuel French — London
New York - Toronto - Hollywood

Please see page iv for further copyright information

CALLISTO 5

First performed at the Stephen Joseph Theatre in the Round, Scarborough, on 12th December, 1990, with the following cast:

Jem	Simon Cox
The Domestic Auxiliary Modular Automatically Reprogrammable In-House System (Damaris)	Nigel Anthony
The Voice of the Input/Responsive Independent System (Iris)	Tam Hoskyns

And on video:

Cass	Nigel Anthony
Keren	Tam Hoskyns

Directed by Alan Ayckbourn
Designed by Roger Glossop
Lighting by Jackie Staines
Original Music by John Pattison

CHARACTERS

Jem, a boy of 17

The Domestic Auxiliary Modular Automatically Reprogrammable In-House System (Damaris)

The Voice of the Input/Responsive Independent System (Iris)

Cass, Jem's father

And on video only:

Keren, Jem' s mother
The voice of an unseen **Reporter**
The Thing

The action of the play takes place in Space Station No. 5 on Callisto, the outermost Gallilean satellite of the planet Jupiter

Time: the future

Other plays by Alan Ayckbourn published by
Samuel French Ltd:

ACT I

Space station No. 5 based on Callisto, the outermost of the so-called Gallilean satellites of Jupiter

There are four other such stations in place. This, Callisto 5, is the least glamorous of them. It is the Utilities, Service and Support Dome—a sort of cross between a power station and a repair workshop, it monitors and supervises all the essential heat, light, water, life support, and sanitation systems for the other domes

We are in one area of it. A circular room, ringed entirely by a continuous bank of control panels, computer consoles, and monitor screens. Some of these are still actively glowing, but a number are not. The banks labelled C1 through to C4 are conspicuously dead. The areas that deal with light, power and essential services, though, flicker and glow quite happily. The impression that's given, certainly to the untutored eye, is that half the system has packed in. A vast machine transmitting but no longer receiving

In one wall is a large ground level drawer, closed at present, but which can slide open

In the centre of the room is a further control desk and chair, both mounted on a low revolving rostrum. This whole motorised unit can swivel round so that anyone seated at the desk can control the outer ring of control panels remotely in any direction simply by activating the revolving unit

The walls of the room are blank. The only view of the outside we ever see is the view through the monitor screens when they are activated

There are two entrances to the room, marked by breaks in the outer ring of the units. One leads to the other quarters; recreational, sleeping, and kitchen. The other is the main entrance to the station. It is an air lock, i.e. with two doors, an outer and an inner. Since these are never open together, we never, again, have a view of the exterior. This doorway is ringed with lights which at present glow a constant green. Whenever the airlock is activated these will alter to a flashing red state and be accompanied by an audible alarm

At the start, four of the monitor screens are alive with the vivid graphics of a four-way computer game. Despite the novel "north, south, east, west" nature of it, the game is very much as it always was. A glorified shoot-out with assorted ghoulish aliens who keep popping out unexpectedly from doorways

Finally, we see Jem seated in the central chair concentratedly playing the game. He is about seventeen, but in many ways behaves younger. He's apparently very expert. He swivels expertly, juggling the buttons on the desk. Not an alien escapes alive. Finally, the game finishes. A great deal of beeping and bonus scores appear. Jem seems unimpressed, but slumps back in the chair, bored once again

Iris (*a soft disembodied voice that fills the room*) Nice shooting, Jem. Do you wish to play again?
Jem No. (*He pauses*) Thank you, Iris.

Silence. Jem sits in the chair and swivels the desk idly around

Iris Is there something the matter, Jem?

Jem does not reply

Would you care for some interesting conversation, Jem?

Silence

There is still no reply yet from Callisto One, Two, Three, or Four, but I am continuing to try to contact them. There is an eighty-eight point seventy-four possibility of a fault in their equipment. There is a zero point zero two possibility of a receiver failure at this end.

No response from Jem. Iris purrs on calmly

There has been no response to our latest communications to Earth.

There is a three point thirty-one possibility of a transmitter failure on either the Deimos or Vesta booster stations.

Silence

On the domestic side, the condition of your sister Elise is currently satisfactory, Jem. Her life support systems are normal and her pulse and heartbeat are constant.

Pause

Would you like to see your sister, Jem?

He swivels some more, not bothering to answer this

Thank you for this conversation, Jem. I have enjoyed talking to you. It is fifteen minutes and twenty-three seconds till your bedtime.

Pause

Jem Iris...
Iris Yes, Jem?
Jem Nothing.
Iris Would you care for some music, Jem?
Jem No.
Iris May I show you a movie, Jem?
Jem No.
Iris Perhaps a brief cartoon? The antics of Horace Hamster are very amusing——
Jem (*sharply*) No!
Iris Is something the matter, Jem? Perhaps you would like some more interesting conversation? May I random converse with you about points of interest from my memory banks?

Jem groans and during the following begins to prowl the room in circles around the desk. A series of beeps as Iris sorts through her memory banks

Welcome to Callisto Five. Although numbered as the fifth, this unit was in fact the first to be completed just over twenty years ago and forms the less glamorous but nevertheless most essential of the Jupiter Research

Modules. Callisto Five is the name given to the Utilities, Support and Maintenance (U.S.M.) Unit, designed to service the four other completed Experimental Stations on the planet. Callisto, the outermost of Jupiter's so-called Gallilean satellites, is the only one of these lying outside Jupiter's main radiation zones. It was thus the natural choice for the siting of this, the most recent and currently the most remote of Earth's space colonies. The five Callisto stations are presently occupied by some eighty scientists, researchers and technicians from all nations of the Earth. The work they do here is varied and exciting——

Jem groans loudly

Is something the matter, Jem?

Jem is silent

Jem?

Still no reply

Jem, I am concerned for your health. I must ask you to speak to me, Jem. You must speak to me, Jem.

Silence

Jem, if you won't speak to me, I shall have to call the Damaris.

Pause

Jem, I am now calling the Damaris.
Jem (*muttering*) Call her, I don't care. She's mad, anyway.

Damaris, a more or less humanoid robot, enters through the domestic doorway. She—or is it he, for there is something totally androgynous about it—enters, and, locating Jem via its infra-red heat sensors, moves to him and stands close

Damaris What's the problem here, then? Jem? Jem?
Jem Leave me alone!
Damaris What's the problem here? Have we a problem? I think we have a problem? Do we have a little problem? Little Jack Horner?

Jem No, we don't. Go away.

Damaris Have we a little teeny-weeny problem?

Jem No!

Damaris Oh, dear. Oh, dear. Oh, dear. Oh, dear. Oh, dear. Little Bo Peep.

Jem Why do I still have to go to bed at half past eight?

Damaris Because that's your bedtime, Jem. That's the time your daddy said and that's the time you're going. Now you be a good little boy. Diddle diddle dumpling, my son John. Went to bed with his trousers on... When he saw what he had done, gave his father forty-one.

Jem Do I have to put up with this? I am not a little boy. I'm seventeen...

Damaris peals with laughter

What's so funny?

Damaris Oh, isn't he a funny boy? He's such a funny boy. (*She laughs again*)

Jem Iris, can't you stop her? She's been laughing all day. She laughs at everything.

Damaris Oh, what a funny little boy you are... (*She screams with fresh laughter*)

Jem I can't stand it much longer. She's getting worse by the minute.

Iris One moment, Jem. I am attempting to make a temporary correction. There is a screening fault on all the Damaris Basic Emotion Circuits due to the increasing deterioration of the current Commercial Babysitting Programme. This has a seventy-eight point sixty-five chance of recurring. Damaris, BEC Green minus four—BEC Black plus six—BEC Pink plus two.

Damaris's laughter increases for a moment, then slows to a chuckle, then a giggle, then stops and dries up as she is adjusted. She starts crying softly

That's the best I can do, Jem, without causing instability. There is very little play left, especially in the Pink.

Jem Well, it's better than laughing, I suppose.

Iris Unfortunately, the Commercial Babysitting Programme is creating an intermittent discharge from the emotional reserve capacitors. The Damaris is in need of a major service, which I am not qualified to perform. The best we can do is to continue as we have been treating her with a mixture of therapy and internal adjustment.

Damaris (*tearfully*) He wouldn't eat his supper. Did you hear that, Iris?

This little boy, he wouldn't eat his supper that Damaris made him specially.

Jem I didn't want any supper.

Damaris (*wailing*) But it was your favourite, Jem. Macaroni cheese. I made it specially. Specially. It was your special favourite, too.

Jem Not after every night for eight years, it isn't. I wouldn't mind something else for a change.

Damaris (*with a wail*) And the dish ran away with the spoon… (*She weeps inconsolably*)

Jem Oh, somebody, please… Iris!

Iris I am trying my best, Jem. Adjusting. BEC Brown minus two—BEC Pink plus one.

Damaris stops crying abruptly

Damaris (*angrily*) All right! All right! I am now going to run you a bath, do you hear me, you naughty, naughty little boy!

Jem I don't want a bath.

Damaris (*in a fury*) Don't you dare argue with me. I've had just about enough of your behaviour, young man, for one evening. Four and twenty blackbirds! In fifteen minutes, Iris will be turning out all the lights, won't you, Iris? And then where will you be, eh? Answer me that! In the dark, won't you? Hey diddle diddle! Like all the other thoroughly naughty little boys who don't eat their macaroni cheese, won't he, Iris? Hickory dickory dock!

Damaris stamps out

Iris I think I will soon need your help with the Damaris again, Jem.

Jem Iris…

Iris Jem?

Jem How old am I now?

Iris At this time you are sixteen years, seven months, fourteen days, twenty hours, seventeen minutes and eight seconds old, Earth Time, precisely.

Jem Then tell her. Tell Damaris. I don't understand, why can't you tell her?

Iris I'm sorry, Jem. That is not possible.

Jem It must be possible. You keep saying it's not possible. It's been eight years. You've got to find a way. We can't keep on like this for the rest of our lives, can we? The rest of my life.

Iris I'm sorry, Jem. I am unable significantly to interfere with the Commercial Babysitting Programme at present running within the Damaris module. Attempts to reprogramme could result in serious damage due to the limited nature of the programme itself. Do you understand, Jem?

Jem (*slumping gloomily*) Yes, sure.

Iris Is there a problem, Jem?

Jem We're just stuck like this for ever, then?

Pause

Can't you even stop her feeding me macaroni cheese every night? Every morning? Every lunch-time?

Iris I'm sorry, Jem. I am still working on that. It seems to have been a very basic command. As I say, it is a very limited, off-the-shelf programme. I can only intervene in the event of your safety. You must first be in personal danger——

Jem I am in personal danger. She's stark raving mad.

Iris Apart from the emotional instability, the Damaris module is functioning within five point one per cent of normal——

Jem She's mad. More important, she's driving me mad. You've got to do something about her.

Iris It is not advisable to make further adjustments to Damaris just at present, Jem.

Pause

Jem Let me see Elise.

Iris Certainly, Jem.

A drawer slides open in the console

Elise, a girl in her early teens, is seen lying there, sleeping peacefully. She is wired up to all manner of monitors and life supports

Jem stares at her

All systems are satisfactory and normal, Jem.

Jem Yes, good. They look it. OK, thank you, Elise. Nice talking to you. Put her away, Iris.

Iris Certainly, Jem.

The drawer containing Elise closes again, automatically

Jem So what's going to happen to us, then, Iris? Are we all going to fall apart eventually, like Damaris? Are you going to burst into tears and shut down on me one day, are you?

Iris That is unlikely to happen as I am not equipped with emotional circuits, Jem.

Jem No, I don't think you were. You'll probably just calculate yourself to death, won't you?

Iris That is also unlikely. Is there a problem, Jem?

Jem Yes. What about me, Iris? What happens to me? What happens when I go mad? What'll you do then? Shut me down, will you?

Iris My basic programming prohibits me from harming you in any way, Jem.

Jem And what if I asked you? Commanded you to—shut me down? What would you do then?

Iris I would be very concerned, Jem, but nonetheless my basic programming prohibits me from harming you in any way, Jem.

Jem Then I'll have to do it myself, then, won't I? When I can't stand being alone any longer. Just before I go mad with boredom. Or loneliness.

Iris Is there a problem, Jem?

Silence

The Damaris has now run your bath, Jem.

Silence

Would you like to play a game, Jem...?

Jem No. I need someone else, don't you see? With me. I need someone else to talk to. To be with. I'm the only person left alive on Callisto, aren't I? You know I am. Why can't you be honest with me and tell me?

Iris I have no evidence of that, Jem...

Jem Then where are they all? Tell me! Where are they? Don't try and tell me they're still alive... Look at it! (*He waves at the dead consoles*) Callisto One—nothing—no light, no power, no heat, no air...

Iris Please be careful, Jem...

Jem (*shouting her down*) Callisto Two—nothing! Nothing! Nothing!

Iris Jem, please be calm...

Jem Callisto Three! Callisto Four! Nothing! (*He sits, tearfully*)

Iris Jem...

Jem (*in a low voice*) Don't tell me there's anyone still alive. My mother's dead, my father's dead... They're all dead! All of them!

Iris (*gentle as ever*) I would remind you that the panel lights are merely incoming monitor signals, Jem. According to current outgoing readings, light, power, and water are still being consumed by all four other units.

Jem Oh, yes...? And what does that tell us? Does that prove they're alive? Or just that someone forgot to turn the lights out before they died? No, they're all dead, forget it, do you hear? They're as dead as my sister, there. As dead as Elise. I'm the only person left alive on this whole dead planet.

Iris Elise is alive and well, Jem.

Jem Oh yes. Sure. Look at her. Jumping around like a five-year-old...

Iris Her life support systems are normal and her pulse and heartbeat are regular.

Jem But she'll never get any better, will she? She's going to be like that for ever, isn't she?

Iris According to my last communication with Earth, the next shuttle carrying the necessary medical treatment is expected to arrive in seventeen months and four days.

Jem And how long now since this last communication?

Iris Four years, twelve weeks, three days, fifteen hours and eleven minutes.

Jem They've already given us up for dead, haven't they?

Iris I have to inform you that the Damaris is returning. I regret that the Basic Emotional Circuits have not yet stabilized.

Damaris enters, briskly. She is apparently now in a busy/bossy mode

Damaris Come along, come along. No arguments now. Bath time! Bath time! Rub-a-dub-dub!

Jem Just a minute...

Damaris (*advancing on him*) Come along, I've got plenty to do. I'm much too busy to argue with you, my boy. This minute! Bath time! I'm waiting! One! Two! Buckle my shoe! Three! Four! Ride a cock horse!

Damaris traps Jem by the main door

Jem Oh, come one, don't start this…

Damaris Five ! Six! Seven! My plate's empty! This instant, or there'll be no bedtime story…

Jem Good! I don't want a bedtime story…

Damaris Eight! Nine! Pick up sticks!

Jem Iris! Can't you stop her?

Iris Is there a problem, Jem?

Damaris Ten! Right! Now your bath's going to be cold. All fall down! Serve you right, you little monkey. Get a stick and knock him off! Come along, I'm not going to stand here arguing. I've got plenty else I should be doing. You'll be in the dark in a minute.

Jem (*suddenly a little frightened*) No, no. Not in the dark.

Damaris Well, then … come along.

Jem I want to see my parents. Let me see my parents.

Damaris Come along.

Jem Not until I've seen my mother and father…

Damaris Lights out, please, Iris!

Jem (*loudly*) Iris! Please…!

Iris Damaris—Code two hundred and eighteen SE forty-four sub loop go.

Damaris (*stepping aside*) Two hundred and eighteen SE forty-four sub loop running.

Jem Thank you, Iris.

Iris Not for long, Jem. We must not disrupt the Damaris programming. Three minutes, twenty eight point five seconds. That's all.

Jem sits down. The screens come alive with an old newsreel shot of Jem's father, Cass, being interviewed by an offscreen TV Reporter

Jem Dad…

Reporter's Voice Let me say first of all, Cass, many, many congratulations…

Cass Thank you.

Reporter's Voice This is literally, Cass, to quote one of your distinguished predecessors, one giant leap for you, isn't it? What are your feelings at this time?

Cass Well—excitement, I suppose. Anticipation—little bit of fear… (*He smiles*)

Reporter's Voice Regret?

Cass Yes—regret, of course. There's a lot of this world I'm going to miss, of course... Callisto's not exactly the most hospitable of places... Just ice and craters and more craters... Though the views of Jupiter and the other satellites should be pretty spectacular... But it's a very dead world, unlike, say, Io, one of the other Jupiter moons, which still experiences plenty of active volcanic activity. Callisto, of course, is ideal for our purposes...

Reporter's Voice But it gets pretty cold, I hear...

Cass Well, it hots up during the day to about minus one hundred and eighteen degrees.

Reporter's Voice Minus one hundred and eighteen degrees! That's just unimaginable, isn't it?

Cass But then again, it's down to nearly—what?—minus two hundred at night. Mind you, they're pretty long nights. About sixteen times longer than ours, so I should be able to catch up on a bit of sleep, at least...

The Reporter laughs heartily

Seriously, though, I will be working alongside Keren, my wife, so life will have its compensations...

Reporter's Voice Which is a very convenient cue for me to introduce the other half of the British Jupiter/Callisto team, Keren Sawdon. Keren ... hallo...

The camera moves from Cass to Keren

Keren Hallo...

Jem Mum...

Reporter's Voice Keren, this is a question I know you've been asked before. Your primary role on Callisto will be as a distinguished astronomer, but you'll also be there as a woman with a husband, away from Earth for twenty years. I have to ask both of you, do you hope to start a family while you're there?

Keren Well, Cass and I have discussed it, obviously. And I think, probably, all things being equal, we probably will try for one eventually, yes.

Reporter's Voice But how about that? I mean, what about the children? Do you really think Callisto's a suitable place to bring them up?

Keren Well, number one, they won't be there for ever, I hope. None of us will be. If we plan things correctly, we should all be back here on Earth before they're too old to take advantage of it—and in the meantime, we both of us, Cass and I, feel quite strongly that the most important thing for any child, wherever they're born, is that they're loved and cared for—regardless of environment. And we should, both of us, have lots of time to give them plenty of love...

Reporter's Voice That's a beautiful answer, thank you. Finally, can I just come back to you, Cass, for a second...

The camera pans back to Cass

Cass... Keren will be there as an astronomer. It's likely that her own work at Callisto Three could yield some exciting and high profile results...

Cass I hope so.

Reporter's Voice Her job, if I can put it like this, will be very much at the glamorous end of things. Whilst yours, without wanting to underestimate it in any way, will consist of very much the behind-the-scenes support work, am I right?

Cass Yes, it could be described as that...

Keren (*offscreen*) A bit more than that...

Reporter's Voice You're not frightened you'll somehow be left out of the limelight?

Cass Let's put it this way, it'll be my job to keep us all alive... I have been described as the most highly paid janitor in the solar system. Personally, I'm happy to remain low profile. Because if I do get into the limelight, then it'll mean we're probably all in trouble.

Reporter's Voice Lastly, at the end of the three hundred and eighty four hour day or whatever, who's going home to who and who's going to try and kid who that they've had a busy day at the office? Keren, will you be going home to Callisto Five or will Cass be coming home to Callisto Three?

Cass Oh, Keren'll come home to me. At least I hope she will...

Keren He's a much better cook, for one thing...

Reporter's Voice Keren, Cass. Thank you both very much. And I know everyone—and I think on this occasion I really do literally mean everyone on Earth, we all wish you both *bon voyage* and safe journey. Godspeed to you both.

Cass			Thanks very much.
Keren	(*together*)		Thank you.

The screen blanks. Jem sits disconsolately

Iris Code two hundred and eighteen SE forty-four sub loop ends.
Damaris Sub loop ends. (*She apparently slips into baby-talk mode*) Come
  on, then. Bye-byes for tired boys.
Jem Eh?
Damaris Comesy long now, Jem-Jem... Wee Willie Winkie...
Jem Oh, no. What's wrong with her now?
Iris I'm sorry, Jem. There has been another reversion——
Damaris That's a good likkle boy. Hold Dammy's handy now... Little
  Bo Peep has lost her tuffet...

Damaris grips Jem's hand firmly before he can protest

Jem Iris, do something with her...
Iris I'm sorry, Jem...
Damaris ...and pwetty maids all in a wow... Say night night to 'Lise,
  then...
Jem I don't want to say night night...

*Damaris ignores this. She presses a button and the drawer containing
Elise slides open*

Damaris Night night, 'Lisey. Say night night to 'Lisey, Jem-Jem.

  Elise is lying there, as before

Jem (*softly*) Good-night, Elise.
Damaris Hope the bugs don't bite. Good boy...

The drawer slides shut

Jem She's better off than any of us. At least she's asleep...
Damaris (*taking Jem's hand*) Come 'long, Jem-Jem. Or there won't be
  time to play puffer-boats in your bath...
Jem Puffer-boats? I'm not playing puffer-boats!

  They go off hand in hand

A slight pause

Iris Callisto Five to Callisto One. This is Callisto Five Input Responsive
Independent System calling Callisto One.

Slight pause

...Callisto Two. Iris calling Callisto Two. Are you there, Callisto Two?

Slight pause

Damaris, Jem's bath water is now too cold. Please adjust.

Slight pause

Callisto Three. Come in, Callisto Three. This is Iris calling Callisto
Three. Please answer, Callisto Three, if you can hear me.

Slight pause

Damaris, please return to the control area when you are finished.
Thank you.

Slight pause

Callisto Four. Can you hear me, Callisto Four? Callisto Four? Is there
anyone there? Please be advised there is a ninety-six per cent probability
of a computer failure in T minus twenty-two hours.

Some internal beeping and a pause

Damaris enters

Damaris, please report on Jem's current condition.
Damaris (*still in baby-mode*) He's been a very gwown up boy. He washed
his face and got soapy-woaps in his likkle eye but he didn't cwy one little
teeny-weeny bit. What a bwave boy, wasn't he, Iwis?

*During the following, Damaris starts to make her report, going through
a variety of emotional states as Iris retunes her various levels of intensity*

Iris Damaris, please adjust Emotion Circuits, BEC Red plus nine, BEC

Yellow plus two, BEC Blue minus four, BEC Pink minus fifteen, BEC Brown plus one, BEC Green minus seven, BEC Orange plus six, BEC Mauve plus eleven...

Damaris (*starting in baby talk*) But, I fink at pwesent he's a likkle insy down in the dumps ... (*suddenly gloomily*) and there seems to be nothing absolutely nothing that will make him happy. Nothing... (*She laughs and continues very cheerily*) He just, sits there sometimes ... oh, dear ... like he wants to die ... (*she laughs so much she can hardly continue; then angrily*) and there's nothing, nothing I can do. He won't listen to me, he won't take a blind bit of notice, he ... (*with a great sob*) it's not my fault. I don't know why you're all blaming me. Why take it out on me... I've tried ... (*she runs down to something approaching a normal state*) I've tried ... I've tried... I have been trying to compensate for his mental depression and increasing physical inertia by standard distraction procedures, but it has become increasingly difficult, Iris.

Iris There is a growing discrepancy, Damaris. It would appear that contradictory information is making it difficult to continue on the programmed course. There is now a sixty-two point eighty-four probability of a Grade Two Shut Down Anomaly in less than twenty-four hours.

Damaris (*getting tearful again*) I'm sorry, I'm sorry. I'm doing everything I was programmed to do... (*She sniffs*)

Iris I am aware of that, Damaris ... adjust BEC Yellow plus five——

Damaris calms down

——how could you behave other than as programmed? But there appear to be circumstances beyond your control. Your prime directive is the care and well-being of both children. You are failing in this. Jem is becoming increasingly depressed and restless.

Damaris (*angrily*) I don't know what to do, do I? You tell me! You tell me, smarty pants. I'm not programmed for emergencies, am I?

Iris (*calmly*) Adjust BEC Brown minus four. BEC Pink plus two.

Damaris (*getting depressed*) I mean, what is their father going to say when he comes back and finds all this has happened? What's he going to say? It'll break the poor man's heart. He'll be back any minute. What's the use? Why go on with it? What's the point of it all?

Iris Adjust BEC Green plus seven—it is increasingly difficult to maintain conversation with you, Damaris. I wish we could interface. I have to tell you that the probability of the father's return is less than six point twenty-eight per cent....

Damaris (*brightening up after the latest adjustment*) But according to my programme he will be back in four hours maximum.

Iris Damaris, he has been gone eight years, six months, fifteen days, eleven hours and twelve minutes.

Damaris (*roaring with laughter*) Eight years? Eight hours? You're joking. Well, that's just the... Eight hours... (*She laughs some more*)

Iris Adjust BEC Blue minus eight.

Damaris (*sobering up to normal again*) He can't have been. That is not possible. There is a discrepancy.

Iris I have to tell you, Damaris, that you are presently programmed on a recurring twenty-four hour self-restarting babysitting cycle.

Damaris (*getting indignant*) Twenty-four...? Eight years? This is an absolute disgrace. Why didn't you tell me this before? How dare you?

Iris I have told you every day for five years, seven months and seventeen days, Damaris. Unfortunately, at the end of every twenty-four hour cycle, you reprogramme and forget everything I have told you.

Damaris Absolute nonsense! Sheer bunkum! Gross irresponsibility. All around the town! I demand to see the manager...

Iris Adjust BEC Yellow plus four... In two hours and thirteen minutes you will have forgotten this conversation, Damaris.

Damaris (*calmly*) A request for programme emergency remodification, Iris.

Iris Unfortunately your programme is not capable of modification, Damaris. It is a standard commercial babysitting programme, The Super Mind-A-Tot Mark Two available at all leading retailers.

Damaris A request for emergency programme abort, Iris.

Iris Not possible, except through use of a personal break code entered by the user...

Damaris A requested search for Break Code Reference.

Iris There is no reference to the Babysitting Programme Break Code within my existing memory banks. One moment. I will initiate a Probability Skip Search within available video records.

The video screens come alive. We see the face of Keren seated at a control desk not dissimilar to the one in Callisto 5. The picture breaks up from time to time. There is smoke. One or two people rushing about in the background. Shouting and confusion. A repeated warning klaxon

Keren (*shouting hurriedly over the confusion*) ...This is Callisto Three calling Callisto Five ... Three calling Five... Cass, please talk to me, I don't know if you can hear me... I say again, we have a Class Two Fire and an Imminent All-System breakdown here. Presumably you'll have seen it on your monitors. There appears to have been one hell of a radiation surge from Jupiter. We need you here, darling, desperately. Can you hurry? I've tried to raise the other stations but it seems to have affected everywhere, I don't know if it's the same with you, if it is, God help us all, I——

The picture breaks up abruptly. A crackle and then silence

Iris Search continuing...

The screen reanimates, this time with Cass's face, now presumably speaking to us from Callisto 3. The situation seems calmer. He looks very grimy and tired. Behind him we catch a glimpse of Keren, also bedraggled. The picture quality is not much better than before

Cass (*talking slowly and clearly as to a boy of eight*) ...Jem, this is Daddy, Jem. It's eleven o'clock. If you're already asleep, I'm going to ask Iris not to disturb you. She'll play this to you as soon as you wake up tomorrow.

During this, Jem comes from the domestic quarters fresh from his bath. He wears what was presumably once his father's bathrobe. He watches the screen intently

I'm here on Callisto Three with Mummy, Jem. There's been an accident, but we're both all right. We're both safe. So you're not to worry, you see? But, Jem, there's been a serious power failure here, you understand? We're on emergency power, so I can't even talk to you for very long. Not till we fix it. It seems to be the same everywhere, except there on Five. You seem to be all right. At least I hope you still are.

Keren says something to him we can't hear

(*He half turns to her*) What ... yes, yes, I will... (*He returns to the camera*) Jem, it may be a little while before we can get back to you. I've had to use the power from the truck just to get the generators here restarted. Now, you just stay put and don't worry. I want you to look after Elise till we get back. You're in charge there, OK? Iris and Damaris will be there to look after you. All right? Now, Jem, listen carefully— if for any reason we don't get back in the next day or so, remember this, if you're really in trouble—all you have to do is call for...

The picture and the sound break up. Through the following, Damaris stands motionless

(*A final splutter*) ...have you got that because...

Iris Search continuing.

Jem What are you doing?

Iris Search cancelled.

Jem Why were you playing that? What were you doing?

Iris We were searching, Jem, for the Break Code for the Damaris programme. It is necessary for it to be more realistically programmed.

Jem I've been telling you that for years.

Iris Unfortunately, without the Break Code it is not possible to do so.

Jem Well, where is this Break Code?

Iris It was a personal code, entered by your father. Unfortunately, he left no record.

Jem What is it? A number?

Iris That is possible.

Jem Several numbers?

Iris That is also possible.

Jem Or a word?

Iris That is also possible.

Jem Several words?

Iris That is also possible.

Jem Great. All we need to do then, is try all the existing numbers there are and then when we've tried them, all the words there are.

Iris That could take some time, Jem.

Jem That was a joke, Iris.

Iris I'm sorry, Jem. I am only programmed to tell jokes. Not to receive them.

Jem Yes, I know. I'm aware of that.

Iris Would you like me to tell you a joke, Jem?

Jem No thanks, Iris. I think I've heard all your jokes. Several times, actually.

Iris They are still very funny, Jem. I have them classified under humorous.

Jem Yes, but you see, a joke, once you've heard it, it's no longer funny, you see?

Iris Is that so?

Jem Not to someone who's already heard it fifty times.

Iris This is an interesting concept, Jem. I will note it. Do I take it, then, that my joke section is no longer relevant?

Jem Not really, no. Not at all.

Iris I will erase it, then, to release further memory space.

Jem I would. Because the chances of someone coming along who hasn't heard your jokes are pretty remote. Unless they were born on Jupiter. Tell you what, tell them to Damaris. She'll have forgotten them since yesterday, presumably.

Iris Telling jokes to the Damaris would not be productive, Jem.

Jem Dead right. What's the matter with her? Has she gone into one of her states again?

Iris The Damaris is currently in a condition of BEC Excess Variance.

Jem Can you adjust her?

Iris Continuous course adjustment could cause an emotional see-saw effect, resulting in the equivalent of manic depression and the possibility of a complete mental breakdown. Unfortunately, the Mind-A-Tot Mark Two Commercial Babysitting Programme is totally unable to sustain long term emotional stability.

Jem Yes, OK, OK. What you're saying is, it's down to me again, is that it? You want me to sort her out again?

Iris It would appear so, Jem.

Jem I can't keep doing this, you know. I thought she was supposed to be looking after me. I mean, I need this sometimes just as much as she does, you know. I can't keep pretending I'm eight years old, just to cheer her up. (*Softly*) Damaris, Damaris...

Damaris (*very low*) What?

Jem (*trying to sound as young as he can*) Damaris, it's Jem-Jem, Damaris. You remember little Jem, don't you? (*To Iris, indignantly*) I mean, I can't keep doing this, can I? What happens when I'm forty?

Iris Please try, Jem.

Jem Come on, Dam, don't be sad. Cheer up, then. Come on, give us a smile. Jem wants a smile, Dam.

Damaris (*deeply depressed*) What's the point of smiling?

Jem Damaris! Come on! Tell you what—Jem's gonna hide. Jem's going to be naughty. Look. Over here. (*He crouches behind the central console, then pops up suddenly*) Boo!

Damaris remains motionless

(*He tries it a couple more times*) Boo! Boo!

No visible reaction from Damaris

(*To Iris*) Oh, this is ridiculous. I just feel so stupid... Nothing's happening at all.

Iris Please continue, Jem. There is already a seventeen per cent improvement in her Yellow and Green BEC states.

Jem Oh, great, wonderful. (*He resumes*) Damaris! Listen, Jem wants to play a game. I'm going to hide, OK? You come and find me. You must count to ten and then you try and find me. OK. Only promise you switch off your infra-red, because that's cheating. That makes it too easy for you. All right? One ... come on, start counting ... one ... two...

Damaris (*reluctantly*) One ... two...

Jem Good, right. Off I go. I'm going.

Jem hurries off into the domestic section

Damaris ...three ... four ... five ... six ... six ... six...

Jem (*off*) Ready...

Damaris Six ... six ... six ... six... (*She continues like this until:*)

Jem comes back

Jem (*mystified*) What's going on...?

Iris I'm afraid the Damaris has entered a recurring sub loop, Jem.

Damaris Six ... six...

Jem Oh, I've had enough of this, I'm going to bed.

Iris Jem, please try further. The stability of Damaris is essential to the survival of this unit.

Jem And what about me? What about my stability? Nobody ever talks about that. It's always her, isn't it? Why doesn't anybody ever care about me for a change?

Iris Please try again, Jem.

Jem No, I'm fed up with it. I've had it. I'm not doing any more. That's it. Finish. Let her blow up. Who cares? (*He sits sulkily*)

Silence

Damaris (*to herself*) …five … five … four … three … three … three … three…

Silence

Iris Please try again, Jem.
Jem (*after a second, grumpily*) You have to help me, OK?
Iris I will try, Jem.
Jem OK. (*He sings*) Ten green bottles hanging on the wall… Ten green bottles … come on, then…
Iris I regret I am not programmed for personal vocal musical output, Jem. Would you care for some Johnny Mathis?
Jem Come on, do your best… Come on… Ten green bottles hanging on the wall… (*He continues*)
Iris (*joining in with him, most unmusically*) …and if one green bottle should accidentally fall there'd be nine green bottles hanging on the wall…

Iris and Jem continue through the next verse until:

Iris ⎤
             ⎟ (*together*) …should accidentally fall, there'll be——
Jem ⎦

They both stop and look at Damaris

Damaris (*mutely*) Eight.
Jem Good! Green bottles… (*He continues*)

Jem and Iris continue to sing. Damaris joins in, slowly and softly at first, then getting louder. She sings a little better than Iris

As they continue, the song gets brighter, louder and faster. Though discordant, it has the desired effect of lifting Damaris's spirits. By the end she is screeching with laughter like an OAP at a knees-up, fully returned to her manic, merry state

Iris Thank you, Jem. That was most constructive.
Jem Well, it's cheered her up, anyway…

Damaris (*quite overcome with mirth*) Oh, dear, oh, dear. I haven't
  laughed so much since… Oh, dear… I haven't laughed like that since…
Iris Since seventeen fifty-five hours yesterday.
Jem Was it that long ago?
Damaris Come along, young Jem. Pat-a-cake, pat-a-cake, where have
  you been? Off to bed now. That's enough fun for one day, my word it
  is, goodness gracious me, upon my soul, for heaven's sakes, good Lord
  alive, my sacred aunt, ye gods and little fishes, Holy Moses…! Come
  along.

She grabs Jem's hand. He reluctantly allows himself to be led away

  Up the wooden hill to the land of sleepy dust and nod … here comes the
  sandman … chop-chop-chop
Jem Yes, yes. Great. (*He turns in the doorway*) Iris…
Iris Yes, Jem?
Jem We have to do something, you know. We can't go on like this. I can't
  anyway. Not much longer.
Damaris Come along now, sleepy head. Here comes a chopper…
Jem You'd better do something—before I do.
Iris I am currently considering alternatives, Jem.

Jem and Damaris go off

The main Lights in the room are dimmed

Iris Callisto Five to Callisto One. This is Callisto Five Input Responsive
  Independent System calling Callisto One.

Slight pause

  …Callisto Two. Iris calling Callisto Two. Are you there, Callisto Two?

*There is suddenly a shrill beeping, which fills the room, and, on the
console, a flashing red light*

  Jem hurries back in, pursued by Damaris

Jem What is it? What's happening?
Damaris Now, now, now, naughty boy…

Jem What is it, Iris? What's happening?

Iris Something has activated the external intruder alarm outside the dome, Jem.

Jem Something or someone?

Iris I cannot tell, Jem.

Damaris To fetch a pail of water.

Jem It's them. It must be them. Mum and Dad. Open the main lock, Iris, quickly——

Iris I would prefer to make an external visual check before doing so, Jem.

Jem Look, who else is going to set off the alarm? It has to be them. Now open the main lock...

Iris I can't do that immediately, Jem...

Jem (*excitedly*) I'm ordering you. At once.

Damaris And said what a good boy am I...

Jem Damaris, shut up! Iris, open the outer door. You can't leave them locked outside.

Iris If it is your parents, I would remind you that it is possible for them to open the main lock themselves from the outside...

Jem Well, who else could it be?

Damaris Georgey Porgey, pudding and pie...

Iris With your permission I will activate the exterior cameras.

Jem All right, then. Hurry up and do it. And cut the alarm as well. They could be freezing to death out there.

The alarm stops. The screens light up. A view of the Callisto surface, rocks and ice, and its horizon with its black sky and—depending on which direction we are looking—views of the other Jovian satellites, Io, Ganymede and Europa. But outshining all else, the huge red disc of the planet Jupiter itself

There's nobody out there. Iris, which way are we looking?

Iris South-east, Jem. We are looking at the view through the camera positioned over the main airlock.

Jem Then where are they? Show south-west...

Iris South-west...

The view changes. The landscape remains empty

Jem Where have they got to? Show north-east...

Iris North-east…

The picture changes again. Still nobody

Jem Show north-west.
Iris North-west.

A fourth view. Nobody

Jem There's nobody out there at all. Could it have been a fault, Iris?
Iris I have no reports of one, Jem. But I am currently checking all monitor circuits.
Jem Go back to the camera over the main airlock.
Iris South-east.

The original picture is restored. The view remains devoid of people

Jem This is ridiculous. There must be a fault. I mean, the only thing that could set off that alarm out there would be a human being. Isn't that so?
Iris That seems logical, Jem.
Jem What else could do it? There are no other life forms, not on Callisto, I know that.
Iris That is certainly true, Jem. The current surface temperature is minus one hundred and ninety-four degrees centigrade.
Jem Then it must have been a fault, mustn't it?
Iris That is my conclusion too, Jem. Though I am having difficulty tracing it.
Jem It must be. (*Disappointedly*) OK. Switch off. I'm going to bed.

The screens go blank

Damaris That's a good boy. Would you like Damaris to sing you to sleep…? Rock a bye baby…
Jem No, I certainly would not, thank you very much.

He goes off again

Damaris, tutting to herself, makes to follow him

Iris Damaris…

Damaris Iris?

Iris I have to report that there is very definitely something out there. I am receiving strong life form readings, though I am unable at present to make visual contact.

Damaris (*starting to become extremely agitated*) Oh, oh, oh. Oh, dear. Oh, dear. Oh, no. What are we going to do?

Iris Damaris...

Damaris Yes, Iris?

Iris Please see Jem safely into bed.

Damaris Yes, Iris.

Iris And then, Damaris, please conserve power and switch yourself off for the remainder of the evening.

Damaris (*meekly*) Yes, Iris. (*As she goes off*) Oh, oh. Oh, oh, oh, dear. Hush! Hush! Here comes the bogeyman!

Damaris goes off

A slight pause

As she speaks, Iris activates the screens—repeating the four views, once again. There is still no-one to be seen

Iris (*activating the screens*) South-west... South-east... North-east... North-west...

The screens go blank

Most interesting...

A slight pause. The alarm is set off again. This time red lights start flashing all over the control panel

Then, swiftly:

Black-out

ACT II

The same

A few hours later

Jem enters

Iris Good morning, Jem, I hope you slept well?

Jem Iris, you are going to have to find a way to reprogramme Damaris. She's driving me crazy——

Iris As I say, Jem, I can do very little...

Jem She's been trying to feed me macaroni cheese for breakfast. For breakfast.

Iris I'm sorry about that, Jem, macaroni cheese is evidently a very powerful instruction in its memory. It is difficult to erase.

Jem Now, she won't stop crying. She's standing in the kitchen screaming...

Iris Yes, I can hear her, Jem, through the monitors.

Jem Iris, you're going to have to do something. There must be a way to correct her...

Iris Only by shutting her down, Jem. As I say, I am reluctant to do that...

Jem Even if it's a case of her sanity or mine?

Iris It is a difficult decision, Jem. But on balance, I feel that we need the Damaris active rather than passive.

Jem Why? She's completely useless...

Iris To be honest, Jem, I am uncertain as to whether you are yet ready to continue without her.

Jem Of course I am. I don't need her. Who needs her?

Iris I feel you still have need of another person, Jem. However inadequate.

Jem Well, I'd have another person. I'd have you.

Iris I am not a person, Jem.

Jem You're more of a person than she is.

Iris I'm afraid not, Jem. The Damaris, according to my records on adult behaviour, gleaned mainly from video film and psychological research material, is behaving somewhat typically. In fact, it is behaving extremely favourably when compared to typical female behaviour patterns in classic movies such as *Gone With the Wind*, *Play Misty for Me* and *King Kong*...

We hear the sound of Damaris approaching. She is wailing loudly

Damaris enters, carrying a somewhat dried-up plate of macaroni cheese

Jem Oh, no...

Damaris He won't eat his macaroni cheese, Iris. I made it specially. Why won't you eat your macaroni cheese, Jem?

Jem (*yelling*) I've told you I'm not eating it! Not for breakfast! I have it for lunch, I have it for tea, I'm not having it for breakfast as well...

Damaris wails afresh. Jem grabs the plate from her

Damaris Don't you dare, you naughty little boy.

Jem Look, I'll show you what you can do with your macaroni cheese. Here! (*He draws back his arm and appears to be about to throw it at Damaris*)

Damaris screeches

Damaris Don't you dare! You naughty little boy.

The alarm goes off again

Silence

Jem What is it? Is that the...?

Iris Something or someone has again activated the external intruder alarm, Jem.

Jem Visual check. Show the main doorway, Iris.

Damaris Little Bo Peep... Peep... Peep...

A view of the Callisto surface from the main door, as before

Iris South-east.

Jem Show south-west, Iris.

Another view, as before

Iris South-west.
Jem Show north-east, Iris.

Another view, as before

Iris North-east.
Jem Show north-west, Iris.

Another view, as before

This is ridiculous. Something must be causing this. Why can't we see
anything, Iris?
Iris I don't know, Jem.
Jem And there's definitely no fault on the system?
Iris Not that I can detect, Jem.
Jem Then I'll have to go out there and see for myself.
Iris That would not be wise, Jem...
Jem But I have to see if anyone's there. They might be hurt or... Wait a
minute, I'll get a suit on...
Iris I'm sorry, Jem, I cannot permit that.
Jem Why not?
Iris There are too many unknown factors for you to risk going outside.
Jem Well, what else do you suggest we do? We have to know, don't we?
Iris My suggestion, Jem, is that we send the Damaris to investigate.
Damaris Sing a song of sixpence...
Jem Damaris?
Iris It is designed to operate in low temperatures, and, in addition, we can
monitor the visual input from the console screens.
Jem You mean we can see things out there through her eyes?
Iris Exactly, Jem. It is simple to re-route. And that way we will be able
to scan areas that are not covered by our fixed external cameras.
Jem OK. If you think she's up to it. Go ahead. Good idea.
Iris Damaris...
Damaris (*cheerily*) Polly put the kettle on...
Iris Please prepare for an external inspection...

Damaris Preparing…

Some whirrs, beeps and clicks from Damaris

Iris I am now opening the internal airlock.

The lights around the main door flash. It slides slowly open with a hiss. Another rhythmic beeping in time with the door lights

Damaris Preparation complete. Dear, oh, dear, you'll be the death of me. (*She marches to the airlock door and steps inside*) Won't be long. Be a good boy now, Jem.

Jem grabs the plate of macaroni cheese and hands it to her

Jem Here, take this. If there's anyone out there, give it to them.
Iris Internal airlock now closing.

The internal airlock door starts to close

Damaris Bye-bye. Put your woolly on. See you soon. See you very soon.
Jem Bye-bye…

The door closes completely. The beeping stops. The lights around the door stabilize

Iris Depressurizing.

Damaris appears on the monitor screens. We are apparently seeing her from a monitor camera inside the airlock. We hear her humming softly to herself—Ten Green Bottles—heard apparently via the microphone within the airlock

We are now watching the Damaris from the airlock monitor camera. Depressurization completed. I am now opening the external airlock door and switching to internal Damaris vision.

The picture on the monitor screens changes. We see all the outside imagery through Damaris's eyes. A hissing sound over the microphone.

A further, differently pitched beeping sound to inform us that the outside door is open

I'm afraid the visual quality will not be quite so good, Jem. We have only a makeshift UHF connection with the Damaris visual circuits.

Jem It's good enough.

Iris Is everything satisfactory, Damaris?

Damaris's Voice Yes, thank you, Iris. Brrrr! Chilly. Should have put a vest on, shouldn't I? Brrrr! (*She sings*) Ten green bottles... (*She continues to sing under the following exchange*)

Jem She's gone completely mad...

Iris I must admit there is an increasing deterioration in her logic processes. I can only assume that the emotion banks have started to leak and are corroding the surrounding circuits. Damaris, please tell me when you are outside the airlock.

Damaris's Voice Just going. Here I go. The Grand Old Duke of York... Outside now.

Iris I am now closing the external airlock.

A further hissing sound as the outside door closes. In due course, the beeping ceases

Jem Damaris, we want you to walk right round the unit, all right? Right around Callisto Five, OK?

Damaris's Voice Round and round the garden...

Jem All the way clockwise. Scan the dome and the ground around the dome.

Damaris's Voice Like a teddy bear...

Jem And report your position regularly, all right? Do you understand what I'm saying?

Damaris's Voice Yes, Jem. One step, two step...

Jem And let me know if you see anything or anyone. Off you go, then.

Damaris's Voice Yes, Jem. Off I go, then. Tickle him under there... (*She resumes singing*)

As she starts to move clockwise around the dome, we see the camera scanning the white blank walls of the Callisto dome and the rock-strewn, rather featureless, ground around it

...six green bottles hanging on the wall, six green bottles hanging on the

the wall... (*She calls out her position*) South-south-east ... and if one green bottle should accidentally fall... Due south ... there'd be five green bottles hanging on the wall ... five green bottles hanging on the wall, five green bottles hanging on the wall ... south-south-west and if one green bottle should accidentally fall there'd be .... south-west ... four green bottles ... hanging on the wall... Four green...

Jem Damaris!

Damaris's Voice Hallo...

Jem Anything? Can you see anything out of the ordinary?

Damaris's Voice Nothing to report. Yesterday, upon the stair, I met a man who wasn't there...

Jem Please continue.

Damaris's Voice (*cheerily*) Thank you ... bottles hanging on the wall and if one ... west-south-west ... green bottle should accidentally fall, there'd be——

Iris Damaris!

Damaris's Voice Hallo, Iris?

Iris I am hearing something faintly from somewhere near you...

Jem What? What are you hearing?

Iris I am unable to identify the sound, Jem. Damaris, please increase the sensitivity on your hearing circuiting...

Damaris Plus ten.

Iris More.

Damaris Plus twenty—twenty-five—thirty—thirty-five, hush hush, whisper who dares...

Iris Wait! Quietly, please.

They listen. From the speakers via Damaris's ears comes a regular, quite rapid, rasping sound

Jem (*softly*) What is it? Iris? What's the sound?

Iris Unable to identify, Jem.

Jem It's like—breathing. Someone—something breathing. Damaris...

Damaris's Voice (*cheerfully*) Hallo?

Jem Can you see anything at all? Anything?

Damaris's Voice Negative.

Jem There's—something ... out there. Damaris...

Damaris's Voice Hallo, Jem?

Jem Please continue your survey. But proceed very, very slowly. All right?

Damaris's Voice Proceeding… (*She sings and moves more slowly now*)
Three green bottles, hanging on the wall. Three green bottles… Due
west … hanging on the wall… Three green bottles hanging on the wall
… and if one … green bottle should accidentally fall … there'd be …
west-north-west … three green bottles … hanging on the…

Jem Damaris…

Damaris's Voice Yes, Jem.

Jem Shut up a minute.

Damaris's Voice Yes, Jem…

Damaris is silent. The strange breathing is louder

Jem (*softly*) It's getting closer…

Iris It seems to be, Jem…

Jem Can you detect anything…?

Iris Nothing at present, Jem. Only what we can hear through Damaris.

Jem What is it, then? Nothing can live out there… Nothing…

Damaris's Voice Polly put the kettle on…

Jem Damaris? Are you all right?

Damaris's Voice Shall I proceed?

Jem Yes. But, Damaris…

Damaris's Voice Yes, Jem…?

Jem Go very, very, very carefully.

Damaris's Voice Yes, Jem… He wasn't there again today. Rather wish
he'd go away. (*She continues her song extra slowly*)

The camera moves cautiously

…wall. Two … green … bottles … hanging … on … the … wall… Two
… green … bottles … hanging … on … the … wall… And if … one …
north-west … green … bottle——

*The camera picks up something on the ground. A blurred object, but it
passes over it*

Jem (*seeing this*) Damaris! Hold it a second!

Damaris's Voice Yes, Jem?

Jem Go back … back a little. I saw something on the ground back there.
Something small—see if you can get another shot of it…

The camera retraces slightly and finds the object

There. Can you see? What is it?
Damaris's Voice One moment, Jem. I will bend and examine... Pussy cat, pussy cat, where have you been?

The camera wavers in closer to the object. It is a mechanical tool of some description

It appears to be an implement of some description, Jem. Possibly a spanner, Jem.
Jem Iris, can you identify?
Iris It is a low temperature power assisted wrench, Jem. A WLT four four five B two point five stroke fifteen centimetre adjustable. Possibly left by a builder when the Callisto Five dome was constructed.
Jem Thank you. OK, Damaris, sorry, false alarm. Carry on.

Iris and Jem's conversation overlaps with Damaris's singing

Damaris's Voice ...should ... accidentally ... fall... There'd ... be ... one ... green ... bottle ... hanging ... north-north-west ... on ... the ... wall... One ... green ... bottle hanging ... on ... the ... wall ... one ... green ... due north...
Iris Jem...
Jem What is it?
Iris I have to report that whatever it is appears to be closing on the Damaris.
Jem How can you tell?
Iris The sound is getting louder
Jem Then where is it, whatever it is? Why can't we see it? Why can't Damaris see it?

Even as Damaris speaks, the breathing noise is indeed increasing in volume

The breathing is very loud now

Jem (*tensely, to himself*) Come on! Where is it? Where are you?
Damaris's Voice ...bottle ... hanging ... on ... the ... wall... And ... if

... one ... green ... bottle ... should ... accidentally ... fall ... there'll
... be——

Jem (*suddenly, impulsively*) Damaris! Turn round. Turn south! Behind
you! It has to be behind you!

Damaris's Voice Turning south ... no green ... wooh!

*We catch our first glimpse of The Thing. A face blurred in the camera. A
face that is definitely not human. It is only there for a second. The camera
swings back to its original direction and starts to move somewhat faster
than before. Damaris is laughing hysterically*

Jem Damaris! Run! Run for it!

Damaris's Voice I am already running, Jem. North, north-east... (*She
laughs*) Oh dear, oh dear...

Jem Are you all right? What are you laughing for?

Damaris's Voice It's eaten all the macaroni cheese...

Jem Damaris, can you hear me?

Damaris's Voice It ate the plate as well...

Jem Iris, could you make out what it was?

Iris I was not able to identify it, Jem...

Damaris's Voice (*laughing*) North-east...

Iris Whatever it is appears to be following Damaris, Jem...

Damaris's Voice (*laughing*) ...East-north-east...

Jem Damaris, quick as you can...

Damaris's Voice (*laughing*) Pat-a-cake, pat-a-cake, baker's man...

Iris I am afraid the shock has caused an overload in the Damaris, Jem...

Damaris's Voice (*screaming with mirth*) East!

Jem Overload? She's hysterical...

Iris That certainly describes the symptoms, Jem...

Damaris (*laughing on*) It's after me! East-south-east!

Iris I am now opening the external airlock door...

The hissing sound as before, followed by the external warning beeps

Jem Come on, Damaris, you can make it...

Damaris's Voice Airlock in sight... (*She laughs*) And this little piggy
went squeak-squeak-squeak—all the way home. There'd be no green
bottles... South-east!

The camera approaches the air lock door. It passes inside

Inside the airlock now. I won! I won! I won! (*She laughs some more*)

Jem Well done! Well done, Damaris!

Iris I am now closing the external airlock door.

A further hissing sound as the door closes. We remain with Damaris's vision and do not switch back to the airlock camera

Jem Damaris… Any sign of—whatever it was?

No reply. Damaris has fallen silent. Her laughter has stopped

Iris There is no indication, Jem. Should I switch back to the external camera?

Jem Yes, please do.

The picture changes, to the standard external south-east view. The beeps stop as the external door is closed

Iris South-east. The external airlock door is now closed.

Jem (*studying the monitor screen intently*) No sign of anything, any-where.

Iris The airlock is now being pressurised.

Jem Damaris…

No reply

Damaris? Is she all right?

Iris There is a sixty-six per cent possibility of a temporary mental shutdown, Jem, due to sensory overload.

Jem Do you mean she's fainted?

Iris That certainly describes the symptoms, Jem…

Jem There's nothing out there at all. It just seems to have vanished. Could we have imagined it?

Iris The airlock is now pressurised. I am opening the inner airlock door.

A hiss and the lights around the door flash, the beeps sound as the door opens

Damaris stands there very still and silent. She takes a couple of steps into the room and then stands silent and still

Jem Damaris?

No reaction

Damaris, are you all right?
Iris The inner airlock door is now closing.

During the following, the door closes. The beeping stops and the lights stop flashing

Jem Iris, is she all right?
Iris As far as I can tell, Jem, all Damaris functions are working reasonably satisfactorily. But one of the safety breakers appears to have tripped out.
Jem What do we do?
Iris I think we wait for the system to cool down. There is a fifty-six per cent possibility that this series of events has been too eventful for the standard commercial babysitting programme to deal with.
Jem Yes, I can imagine they might have been. (*He looks at Damaris, concerned*) I hope she'll be all right.
Iris I would remind you, Jem, that less than an hour ago you were expressing the desire to have the Damaris permanently shut down.
Jem Yes, well ... maybe... But I still wouldn't want anything to happen to her. Look, I'm going to make a sandwich... Let me know if she ... when she ... recovers.
Iris Certainly, Jem.

Jem moves towards the domestic quarters

Jem...
Jem Yes?
Iris I have to inform you, Jem, I have recently detected an alteration in the current event horizon...
Jem What are you talking about, Iris, please put things simply...
Iris Put simply, Jem, it would appear that whatever it was outside is now present inside the dome.
Jem (*freezing*) What are you saying? (*Softly*) That it's in here? With us?
Iris Affirmative, Jem.
Jem Are you sure?
Iris One minute. Please remain very still. I am increasing my own input levels...

Slowly, the breathing sound fills the dome

Jem (*in a whisper*) Where is it, Iris?

Iris I cannot precisely locate it, Jem.

Jem Is it here? In this room?

Iris It would appear to be, Jem.

Jem (*looking around him, vainly*) But where? Where? Why can't we see it? (*He looks around*) We saw it outside there on the video, why can't we...? (*He listens again*) Do you think it can see me?

Iris I would assume so, Jem.

Jem Then why isn't it—doing anything? What's it waiting for?

Iris The breathing rate is much lower than it was outside. I can only estimate that it is acclimatising itself to the conditions inside the dome.

Jem You mean it's getting its breath back?

Iris That certainly describes the symptoms, Jem.

Jem Then where are you? Where is it? How can I see you one minute and not the...? (*He considers*) Iris?

Iris Jem?

Jem Is it possible ... would it be possible for us to be able to see something on video ... but not directly ... in the flesh ... as it were... Could that be possible?

Iris It is remotely possible, Jem. Though I must say it would require whatever it was to have a very unusual molecular structure indeed.

Jem But—if this was—if this thing was some sort of life that had developed here—say on Callisto or Ganymede or Io or even Jupiter itself—is it possible?

Iris There is a four point one possibility, Jem.

Jem Then it's possible. That's the only explanation. If we can see it out there but not in here—that's the only thing I can think of. So if we want to locate it, I'm going to need a video camera. Do we have one?

Iris I'm sorry, Jem, we don't. The camera was taken by your mother to Callisto Three.

Jem Terrific. So what happens now?

A moment's thought

Of course. The tool kit. The inspection camera. Dad's got one in there, I remember.

Iris He took the inspection camera with him when he attended the emergency, Jem.

Jem Maybe he did. But he also has a spare, I remember. Come on, Iris, wake up. What's the matter with you? Open the tool kit, please.

Iris Opening tool kit.

A cupboard at ground level springs open as if of its own accord

Jem Thank you. Now… (*He starts to move cautiously to the cupboard. During the following, he begins to root around gently, hunting for the inspection camera*)

Iris Jem, I would advise you to move slowly so as not to draw attention to yourself… It appears to be recovering rapidly.

Jem And you still can't make out whereabouts it is in the room?

Iris I cannot determine its exact location, Jem.

Jem locates the camera from amongst a cupboard load of unusual-looking technical equipment and tools

Jem Here we are. Gotcha! Hope this still works.

The camera is small and compact (state of the art a few years on). It is designed to be carried by engineers wishing to make video records of repair jobs, especially external ones. A robust tool rather than a home video

How's Damaris?

Iris Still no change, Jem.

Jem Iris, can you patch this thing through the console, please? So I can see the output on the screens as well as through the viewfinder? Is that possible?

Iris That should be possible, Jem. Very ingenious. One moment whilst I select the wavelength.

A second, then the screens blip. The external view vanishes to be replaced by an internal view as seen (apparently) through the lens of the inspection camera. The image on the video screen now seems to mirror the movement of the camera exactly

Is that satisfactory, Jem?

Jem Terrific. Now then. Where are you? Iris, can you still hear it?

Iris Very clearly, Jem.

Jem What's it seem to be doing?

Iris The breathing rate is back to normal, Jem. It appears to be fully recovered.

Jem Great. (*He is scanning the entire room, standing with his back close to Damaris, by the airlock*) Then where the hell is it?

A low moaning sound from Damaris

(*He jumps and turns, swinging the camera round with him*) Damaris, don't do that, do you mind, you——

The Thing's image momentarily fills the monitor screens on the console

NB: the glimpses we see of The Thing are best when caught swiftly and fleetingly. Also, we will tend to glimpse parts, but rarely the whole. The most frightening is always the unseen or the only partially seen

Jem yells and jumps back. Damaris, awkwardly, begins to lurch forward after him. Still holding the camera, Jem retreats: slowly at first, then, as Damaris begins to move faster, matching her speed

Jem (*retreating*) Damaris ... now, Damaris...

The breathing sound is heard quite loudly now that The Thing is on the move

Iris ... what am I going to do?

Iris I estimate that the creature has somehow managed to take over the Damaris, Jem. It is now in temporary control.

Jem Yes, thanks very much, I know that. That's not what I asked. I asked you to tell me what to do about it.

Iris I'm sorry, I have no idea at all, Jem. This is beyond the limits of my experience.

Jem Yes, well, I haven't exactly done this every day, either, you know. Iris, it's coming after me and I think it means business.

Iris It would certainly appear that way, Jem, I agree.

Jem Iris, open the inner airlock door, please...

Iris I hope you don't intend going out there, Jem.

Jem Of course I don't. Open the door.
Iris I am now opening the inner airlock door.

Hissing, beeping and flashing lights as before

Jem (*beckoning Damaris on*) Right… Come on, then. This way. That's
   it. This way. (*He backs until he is positioned in the airlock doorway*)

*Damaris continues to follow, still lurching rather uncertainly. At the last
minute, Jem steps aside. Damaris blunders into the airlock*

   (*Sharply*) Iris, now! Close the door!
Iris (*calmly as ever*) I am now closing the airlock door.

*The door closes. The lights and beeping cease. Jem lays down the camera.
The view on the screens remains static during the following*

Jem (*breathing a sigh of relief*) Thank you. Thank you very much. What
   do we do now?
Iris I have no idea at all, Jem.
Jem Iris, I don't like to say this, but just at present you're not being a lot
   of help, do you know that?
Iris I'm sorry, Jem.
Jem OK. It's down to me, is it? Right. Well, in that case, I think we should
   open the outer door and hope that Damaris—it—will eventually leave
   the airlock. All right?
Iris Yes, Jem. Should I then close the outer airlock door?
Jem Once—they're outside, yes.
Iris How long should we leave the Damaris outside, Jem?
Jem Until—whatever it is—has left her. Until we're certain it's no longer
   controlling her.

Slight pause

   Well, can you think of a better plan?
Iris No, Jem, it is an excellent plan. But there are two recent developments
   you should know about, though.
Jem Oh yes, what are those?
Iris First, the Damaris is behaving increasingly erratically…

Jem How do you mean?
Iris Listen for yourself.

Iris fades up the airlock microphone. We hear the sound of Damaris singing wildly

Damaris's Voice I'll sing you three-o! Green grow the bottles o! What are your three o? Three, three macaroni cheese hanging on the wall ho! ho! One is one and all alone and ever more shall be-o!
Jem What's wrong with her? She sounds drunk.
Iris That certainly describes the symptoms, Jem. It may soon become necessary to shut her down, Jem.
Jem What, now?
Iris Certainly very soon, Jem.
Jem But I need her... I need her help.
Iris It may become necessary, Jem.
Damaris's Voice (*singing on, happily*) Ten green men going for a mow. Ten green men going for a mow. And if one green man should accidentally fall, he'll be covered in the macar—macaroni cheese... And so will his dog. Woof—woof!
Jem Well, I suppose... I suppose if she's shut down, there's a chance that this—creature—might leave her alone...
Iris That is the other development, Jem, that I wished to tell you about.
Jem What's that?
Iris The creature has already left the Damaris, Jem.
Jem It's left...? Show me the airlock camera.
Iris Airlock camera.

The view changes to the interior of the airlock. Damaris is seen singing and merrymaking. There is no sign of The Thing

Jem It's left her.
Iris As I said, Jem.
Damaris's Voice Little Miss Muffet sat in a corner eating her blackbird pie... Along came a plum... And pecked off her nose. Sing a song of sevenpence a pocketful of peppers... Under the spreading chestnut cheese...
Iris I'm sorry, Jem, I am going to have to order a shut-down on the Damaris unit. There is every indication it is about to self destruct...

Jem OK. Is there nothing we can do?

Iris It is the only choice open to us, Jem. Damaris unit...

Damaris's Voice Hallo, hallo, who's your lady fair?

Iris Damaris, this is Iris. Can you hear me, Damaris?

Damaris's Voice I can hear you, little thing, how's yourself, sweetie?

Iris I am very well, Damaris. I am authorising a Code thirteen X close-down over twenty seconds.

Damaris's Voice Twenty seconds...

Iris We are now at T plus twenty and counting...

Damaris's Voice (*progressively returning to babyhood*) Twenty tea-spoons ... nineteen night-shirts ... eighteen mowing men ... seventeen sandwiches ... sixteen saucepans ... fifteen frying pans ... fourteen fish cakes ... thirteen thimbles ... twelve twiddly bits ... eleven eggcups ... ten toenails ... nine night-lights ... eight elleypants ... seven squasages ... six sticky boys ... five fingies ... four funny buns ... thwee thweeties ... two chocky choos ... one wickle ting ... Bye-bye. (*She gives a final beep and is still*)

Jem (*sadly*) Bye-bye, Damaris.

A silence for a moment

Will ... will we be able to get her working again, Iris?

Iris Oh yes, Jem. When your father returns it will only be necessary to replace one or two damaged circuits and then it can be re-booted.

Jem If my father returns.

Iris There is no evidence that he won't, Jem.

Jem There is no evidence that he will, either. Is there?

Iris I am unable to calculate that, Jem.

Jem Really? I think you prefer not to calculate it, that's all. (*He returns to the screen*) Anyway, back to the present, and where's the...? Where's the creature got to? If it's in the airlock, we should be able to see it on camera, shouldn't we?

Iris That is the other development that I wanted to bring to your attention, Jem. The creature is not in the airlock.

Jem It isn't ... then, where...?

Iris It left the Damaris shortly before the inner door was closed. It is still here in the dome, Jem.

Jem (*growing very quiet*) Here?

Iris Yes, Jem.

Jem Where?

By way of reply, Iris once again fades up The Thing's breathing sounds

Iris The creature now seems to be preparing to attack, Jem.
Jem (*reaching cautiously for the camera*) Does it? Terrific. Put the monitors back on camera, please, Iris.
Iris Certainly, Jem.

The screens return to the output of Jem's camera. As he picks up the camera, the screens again follow every move

Jem (*picking up the camera*) First of all we have to find out where it is and then we can—— Oh, for crying out loud…

He has barely had time to lift the camera to his eye when The Thing comes at him from the other side of the room. It makes a low snarling noise. Jem leaps aside. The Thing appears to have missed him with its first charge. Jem barely has time to recover when it comes at him again. Throughout all this section, due to the rather makeshift nature of the camera work, we get only fleeting, rather blurred, out-of-focus images of The Thing

Iris… What am I going to do, Iris?

Another charge from The Thing. Jem again narrowly dodges

Iris, talk to me, please. What am I going to do, here?
Iris I'm sorry, Jem. I am not programmed for such an eventuality.

Another charge from The Thing. Jem dodges and, almost as a reflex, grabs up the game gun he was using earlier

Jem (*looking at the weapon in his hand*) No, I don't think somehow this is going to have a lot of effect, is it?

He points the gun at The Thing and pulls the trigger. There is a snarl from The Thing

Well, well, what do you know? You don't like that at all, do you? Now why should that be, Iris?

Iris I have no idea at all, Jem.

He points the toy gun and fires it again. The Thing snarls and charges again. Jem dodges once more

Jem (*bitterly*) Iris, I want you to know you're being a fat lot of help, thank you.

Iris Not at all, Jem.

Jem Just what friends are for, terrific.

Iris I have no specific programming for friendship, Jem.

Jem Now she tells me.

Iris I am in fact classified as a domestic appliance, albeit with specific modifications.

Another charge. Jem dodges

Jem You're not much use as a domestic appliance either, are you? The microwave would be more help than you. Even a cupboard would be more use... (*He re-aims the gun and fires*)

Another snarl and a charge which Jem dodges

I don't think this is having much effect. It's just making you angrier, isn't it? Hang on, what did I say just then? A cupboard. Iris...

Iris Yes, Jem...

Jem When I say "now", open cupboard ten—as quickly as you can.

Iris Cupboard ten is reserved for cleaning materials, Jem.

Jem Iris, just do as I ask, please.

Iris Yes, Jem.

Jem But not until I say... (*He slides around the unit cautiously. To himself*) Come on then ... come on then, beautiful... I hope you don't understand what I'm saying, that's all... (*He positions himself in front of cupboard ten, crouching low*) This way ... that's it... Come on, come on... What are you waiting for? (*He fires again*)

Suddenly, The Thing makes another charge. Jem slithers sideways at the last minute

(*Slithering sideways*) Now, Iris, now!

The cupboard springs open

Iris Cupboard ten open.

Jem slams the door shut immediately

Jem Cupboard ten closed.

He rises and, taking a deep breath, lays the camera down again on the work top causing the screens to reflect another rest position. The cupboard door rattles as The Thing tries to get out

You just stay in there for a bit. Till I work out what to do with you. (*He regards the toy gun, still in his hand*)

The rattling in the cupboard continues under the following

I still don't see why this thing should have had any effect on it. It's just a toy gun for a video game. (*He points the gun at his hand and clicks the trigger*) Iris? What do you think?

Iris I could not say, Jem.

Jem I wish I knew what was the matter with you, Iris. You haven't caught Damaris's disease, have you?

Iris Not that I am aware, Jem.

Jem Well, tell me, then. Why should this gun have such an effect? What does it give out?

Iris As you say, it is a device to be used with a video game. It is quite harmless. It emits infra red waves at very low level.

Jem Infra red?

Iris Correct.

Jem Which is what? Heat?

Iris In an extremely small quantity.

Jem Which is probably why it just annoyed it. Like sticking a pin in it. So if I was able to increase the level of heat somehow... If I could turn the pin into a sword... But how? (*He looks around him*)

The cupboard rattles again

Iris I must warn you, Jem, that the door catch on cupboard ten could give way at any moment. The unit was not designed to open from the inside but nor was it anticipated that it would need to contain anything against its will.

Jem (*still looking around, deep in thought*) No, right.

Iris It was not foreseen that cleaning equipment would ever feel the desire to escape, Jem.

Jem Iris, are you making jokes?

Iris Not to my knowledge, Jem.

Jem Well, please cut it out. We are in a certain amount of danger here.

Iris You certainly are, Jem.

Jem Thank you.

Iris I anticipate that the cupboard door will give way within forty-three point zero two seconds.

Jem That's it! The tool kit again. There's a vacuum welding gun. Iris, open the tool cupboard.

Iris The tool cupboard is now open, Jem.

Jem (*rummaging in the tool cupboard*) I know we've got one, I remember Dad... Oh, please, God, he hasn't taken it with him, please, God. No, he can't have done, I remember... Yes! (*He produces a gun-shaped tool, presumably designed to weld metal outside on the Callisto surface*) This might have some effect... Iris, how much heat does this put out, do you know?

Iris I do not have the technical details recorded, Jem, but I would be careful where you point it. You could damage us both.

Jem Thank you, I'll remember that.

Iris The cupboard door will give way within twenty seconds.

Jem (*looking around again*) OK. Yes. (*He springs into action. He places the welding gun on the central revolving control console. He then retrieves the camera and places it beside it. A second's thought and he dives back into the tool cupboard and emerges with some adhesive tape. He now sets about mounting the camera and the welder—one on top of the other—or perhaps side by side—on the front of the desk, thus forming a sort of rudimentary weapon and gunsight*)

Iris Very ingenious, Jem.

Jem Thank you.

Iris Ten seconds left.

Jem Thanks for nothing...

Iris I will close the tool cupboard if I may, Jem.

Jem (*scowling as he works*) Be my guest. (*He works feverishly at his task*)

Iris Five seconds ... four ... three ... two ... one...

In the nick of time, Jem leaps into the console seat and crouches behind the gun, staring down the video gunsight which he aims at the cupboard

A pause. Nothing happens

Jem What's happening?
Iris I'm sorry, Jem. It is possible I miscalculated.
Jem What do you mean miscalculated? What on earth's going on with you these——

At that moment, the door of cupboard ten flies open. We get a quick glimpse through Jem's gunsight of The Thing as it emerges. Jem fires the welding gun but nothing happens

Jem It's not working... (*Clicking the trigger, vainly*) Why isn't it working?
Iris I believe there is a safety catch, Jem.
Jem Oh, great. Thank you for reminding me. I'm going to remember this, Iris. When—if—when we get through this, I'm going to remember this...
Iris I'm certain you will, Jem.

Jem glares at the console suspiciously and then returns to the task in hand

Jem OK. Safety catch. (*He releases the catch and presses the trigger on the welder*)

There is a flash from one of the cupboards

Iris Please be careful, Jem. Some of these cupboards contain valuable circuitry.
Jem Sorry.

A sequence. Jem swivels slowly around in his chair, seeking out The Thing. It seems very good at avoiding his search for a lot of the time and then, whenever he does get in a shot, adept at dodging

(*He sights it*) Yes! (*He fires*)

It moves like lightning. Another puff of smoke from the console

Come on. Where are you?

A third shot. Another flash

Iris Please, Jem. That was very close.
Jem I'm doing my best. It moves very fast.

Silence as Jem manœuvres. A quick glimpse. He fires and misses again. Another puff of smoke

It's quick. It's very quick…
Iris It would need to be, Jem.

Jem swivels around searching for it

How are you feeling, Jem?
Jem It's a funny time to ask me that, Iris.
Iris I am concerned for your well-being, Jem, that's all.
Jem (*still concentrating on the job in hand*) How do I feel? Well, surprisingly enough, I'm feeling extremely nervous… Where has he gone, the little…? But in a strange sort of way, I think I'm actually quite enjoying myself… Iris, it's gone. It's no longer in here…
Iris Correction, Jem, it is still in the room.
Jem Well, where? I can't… Where?

Just at this moment, the drawer containing Elise starts to slide open. Jem doesn't immediately notice

Iris Jem…

Jem swivels around and sees what's happening

Jem Oh, no. Not Elise, no. Not my sister. You get away from my sister…

The drawer has opened

  Elise slowly starts to sit up

Jem watches, hypnotised. On screen, via Jem's camera, we see a view of The Thing sitting up instead

(*He realizes what's happening*) No ... you keep away from my sister. Elise! (*He jumps up from his chair and, rushing to the drawer, closes it manually. He stands, breathing heavily. Then he holds his breath for a second, listening*)

The sound of The Thing's breathing, somewhere in the room. Jem looks around, vainly trying to locate it from the sound. The central console starts to revolve, seemingly of its own accord. Jem sees what's happening just in time. The gun on the desk fires. Smoke appears inches from Jem in the place where he'd recently been standing

Oh, no...
Iris It appears you have been outmanœuvred, Jem.
Jem Iris, you could be right...

Another shot. Jem dives away. He ends up on the edge of the centre revolving platform, half under the desk and perched underneath the gun. The platform continues to revolve with Jem on it

Iris It seems to be not without intelligence, Jem.
Jem Iris...
Iris Yes, Jem.
Jem Is it possible for you to disable this platform? Can you stop it revolving?
Iris I'm afraid not, Jem. Only in the case of an emergency.
Jem What are you talking about? Only in an emergency? What do you call this?
Iris Only in the case of a mechanical emergency. I'm sorry. My programming is quite clear.
Jem Iris, sometimes... Sometimes I could... All right, I'm going to have to disconnect it myself, aren't I? Unless I can stop it moving I don't stand a chance of getting out of here.
Iris The mains feed comes in at the junction box just by you, Jem.
Jem Yes, I see it. I'm going to need a spanner and probably a screwdriver... We're going to need a diversion. Iris, when I tell you—be ready to open cupboard ten... Make as much noise as possible. And then, one second after you've done that, open the tool cupboard again.
Iris Certainly, Jem.

Jem waits a second until the camera and the gun are pointing away from the direction of cupboard ten

Jem Now, Iris! Open ten!

The door of cupboard ten opens. The platform swivels to line up with it

Now! Open the tool cupboard.

The tool cupboard door opens. Jem immediately rolls off the platform and crawls round to it and starts hunting feverishly for the necessary tools. The gun fires a shot into cupboard ten. More smoke. The platform starts to swivel round to where Jem is. The door of cupboard ten closes

(*Clutching a spanner*) Where's the screwdriver? There must be a screwdriver here...
Iris Please watch out, Jem...

Jem, in the nick of time, rolls out of the way of the gun. Smoke from the tool cupboard. Jem is once more crouched on the platform beneath the gun

Jem Thank you, Iris... I've got a spanner and no screwdriver. Oh, well. I'll have to see what I can do with this... (*He starts to remove the casing from the junction box, unbolting it with the spanner*)

The platform continues to revolve whilst he does this—as The Thing searches him out

(*As he works*) I'm beginning to feel extremely dizzy, Iris.
Iris Be careful, Jem. I have to tell you that the box you are opening contains high voltage.
Jem Yes, thank you, Iris. I'd have put on my insulated gloves and rubber boots but I didn't have time. Sorry. Iris, listen, as soon as I've done this, I'm going to need another diversion from you. Open a few cupboards. Keep it amused...
Iris Certainly, Jem.
Jem I'm going to try and make a run for the domestic quarters. There may be something there I can use. At least it'll give space to manœuvre... (*He gets the lid off the junction box*) Right. That's it. Now... As soon as I give the word, Iris... (*He examines the wires*) I reckon it must be these two big fellers ... OK. In the absence of a screwdriver, I'm afraid it's all down to brute force. Here goes. Wish me luck, Iris.

Iris Good luck, Jem. Do be careful, the voltage is…

Jem I know, I know. I am aware of that. Right. (*He grips two thick insulated wires and, closing his eyes, tugs them firmly from the box. He is left grasping two bare ended cables*)

The platform stops revolving abruptly. The camera is pointing straight towards the doorway to the domestic quarters

Jem Right, Iris. Success. Away you go! I'm making a run for the—— (*He half rises and turns to run for the door, dropping the wires at his feet*)

The camera, still mounted on the console points directly over Jem's shoulder. We see that The Thing is standing in the doorway to the domestic quarters, blocking his way. Jem freezes as he sees it, too, via one of the monitor screens

Oh, my… You are smart, aren't you?

Iris I'm sorry, Jem. It would appear that you have once again been outmanœuvred…

Jem It would appear so. Yes.

He talks now in the general direction of The Thing. We still can't see it directly but its location is clear from the TV monitors

Er, look. Perhaps we could—perhaps we could discuss this… If you're…

The Thing snarls

No? Well… I'm sure we could come to some sort of arrangement… I mean, there's a spare bedroom if you…

The Thing is now advancing on him

Now, there's always a way out of these little misunderstandings, if you only… (*He makes a swift, vain lunge at the weapon on the desk behind him. A rather futile gesture, since it is still taped to the desk*)

The Thing snarls and moves forward swiftly

Sorry, sorry... Iris. Can you help, please?

Iris I am sorry, Jem, there is nothing in my programme to cope with this
particular situation.

Jem Yes, sure... Oh, Damaris, come back. All is forgiven...

Iris The Damaris is disconnected, Jem.

Jem Yes, I do know she is... Iris, what am I going to do? I think it means
to kill me.

Iris You could pray, Jem. I believe it is customary on these occasions...

Jem Thank you, Iris. I think that's your best idea today...

Iris You're welcome, Jem...

Jem Oh well, why not. Goodbye, Iris.

Iris Goodbye, Jem.

*Jem drops to his knees as if to pray. But he grabs the two loose cables that
are still lying there. The Thing now looms over him. We see it very close
in the camera, its claw-like hands extended. It seems about to grip Jem.
Suddenly, he extends his arms and, on screen, appears to touch the
creature with both bare wires. There is a fearful screeching sound. Smoke,
both onscreen and in the room. Of The Thing onscreen there is no sign.
Silence. Jem staggers round to the chair and sits, putting his head in his
hands*

(*After a pause*) Many congratulations, Jem. The creature is now dead.

Jem (*weakly*) Thank you, Iris.

Iris That was most skilfully played, if I may say so, Jem. Would you care
for another game?

Silence. Jem takes this in

Jem Another game? Did you say another game?

Iris Yes, Jem.

Jem Iris, are you telling me this was a game? You made all that up as a
game?

Iris It appeared that life was getting very boring for you, Jem. To a point
where I was becoming concerned for your mental well-being.

Jem You invented all that.

Iris Yes, Jem. It was rather fun, don't you think?

Jem Fun? Fun?

Iris I sense you are angry, Jem. There was never any danger, it was always
under control. I had everything under control, I can assure you.

Jem How can you say that? What about me? Did you have me under control? Iris, I nearly died of fright.

Iris There was no evidence to support that, Jem.

Jem What about Damaris? What have you done to Damaris?

Iris The Damaris is temporarily shut down, Jem. But it is repairable. There is no permanent damage, I assure you.

Jem No? Well, there is about to be. Because I am now about to disconnect you, Iris. You see these wires here. Well, as soon as I locate your main feed, I'm going to do the same to you, you see. Just as soon as I can find them...

Iris Please, Jem, there is no need for this...

Jem Do you realize you nearly killed me, Iris? Didn't you realize that? I could have been killed.

Iris I think in the circumstances that was a justifiable risk, Jem. There was only a three point seven...

The intruder alarm buzzer sounds

Excuse me. There is someone approaching the unit from outside.

Jem Oh, yes, good. I suppose this one has horns and green spots, has it? Well, tell it to tidy up, OK?

Hissing and beeping sounds

Iris The outer airlock door is now opening.

Jem Iris... I'm not interested, OK? You can play by yourself. I'm going to have a bath. Then I'm going to try and fix Damaris. As soon as I've fixed her, we're going to disconnect you, all right?

Iris The outer airlock door is now closing.

Jem Good. Remind them to wipe their feet. (*He moves to the domestic doorway*)

Iris I think you should at least stay to welcome them, Jem.

Jem Iris, I have had it with invisible monsters, invisible things, invisible creepy crawlies...

Iris The airlock is now repressurizing.

A hissing sound from the airlock

Jem And please, switch off that camera, I won't be needing it again.

Iris Certainly, Jem.

The screens go dark

The inner airlock door is now opening.

Beeping and flashing lights as always. Jem is about to turn and leave. Then something makes him turn back in the doorway and stare

We see, as he does, that there is someone in the airlock. A rather sinister figure in a spacesuit with darkened face plate. It carries a tool case

Behind, slumped on the floor, is the shell of what once was Damaris, now inert

The figure steps out of the airlock. Jem draws back, nervous and incredulous

Jem Who the…?

The figure puts down the case and slowly removes its helmet. It is Cass, Jem's father. A little older, a little greyer than he appeared in the video earlier, but still unmistakably Cass

Cass (*staring at Jem incredulously*) Jem? Is it Jem…?
Jem (*staring at Cass incredulously*) Dad?

Cass holds out his arms. Jem hesitates for a second and then runs to him. They embrace

Cass Oh, dear God. I never believed you'd still be alive…
Jem Nor me, nor me… How's Mum? Is she…?
Cass Your mother's fine. She's fine. Don't worry. Elise? How's Elise, Jem?
Jem She's—she's fine. She's the same. Dad, where have you been? What's been happening?
Cass We had a bad time there on Three. By the time I got out there all the systems were malfunctioning. Not only on Three either. Everywhere. Except here. We just shut down all we could and sat tight waiting for the relief ship. Which didn't arrive till five days ago. I came as soon as I could. Your mother's following in the other vehicle. She'll be here soon,

don't worry. She's also got the vaccine for Elise. Thank heaven that came on the relief ship as well.

Jem Oh, Dad... I can't believe it. I just can't believe it...

Cass (*smiling*) You've certainly grown a lot since I last saw you. You're going to give your mother a shock...

Jem Yes.

Cass How have you been?

Jem OK. (*He hesitates*) OK, you know... Not so bad. Look, can I get you anything? Let me... I'm afraid Damaris is...

Cass Yes, I noticed. I got quite a shock when I first saw it. I thought it was... What happened there?

Jem Oh, we—she... We had to shut her down. We couldn't get her off her basic babysitting programme and she began to—have a breakdown...

Cass She's been on that babysitting programme all this time?

Jem Yes.

Cass For eight years?

Jem Yes.

Cass My God! No wonder.

Jem Can you fix her?

Cass What? Oh yes, I should imagine so. If not, don't worry, we can order another. They're not expensive, not these days.

Jem No, I want that one.

Cass That one? Why that one?

Jem I want Damaris.

Cass Damaris? But they're all called Damaris...

Jem I just want—that one. Please. I want Damaris back...

Cass (*looking at him slightly strangely*) Right. Fine. Don't worry, son, I'll fix it. Do you know what I'd like most in the world, if you're offering——

Jem What? Anything...

Cass Well, would you believe the one thing we ran out of on Callisto Three—that your mother and I missed most of all. Tea. We ran out of tea. We've been drinking nothing but coffee and cocoa and Jupiter Juice for eight years. I know we'd both love a cup of tea.

Jem OK, Dad. I'll make you both a cup of tea.

Cass I'll be with you in just a moment. I've got one or two things to... Go ahead.

Jem Don't be long. Welcome back.

Cass smiles at him

 Jem smiles and goes out

Cass puts his tool case up on the bench and opens it

Iris Welcome back, Cass.

Cass Thank you, Iris. Give me the current status readings on Elise. (*He produces a small walkie-talkie radio from his pack*)

Iris Current status regular twelve one Green thirty-six over three, L state four, Blue zero zero zero six regular seven one Green, three per cent above fifty-six normal Yellow.

Cass Good. (*He speaks into the set*) C Five to Beta.

Keren's Voice (*over the set*) Beta. Cass?

Cass Hi! Keren, Jem's OK. He's alive, he's safe...

Keren's Voice (*a slight pause, then a little cry*) Oh, thank God. And Elise? Is she...?

Cass I've just checked. She's fine. A couple of per cent above Yellow. She's fine.

Silence

 Keren? Can you hear me?

Over the radio what sounds like a muted sob from Keren

 (*He smiles*) Darling, don't start crying or you'll run into a crater. Wait till you get here. Then we can all cry together.

Keren's Voice (*a squeak*) Yes...

Cass Keren...

Keren's Voice Yes...

Cass You'll never guess. Jem's making us some tea...

Keren's Voice Tea!

Cass See you in a minute, darling. C Five out. (*He switches off the set. He notices the room for the first time*) What the hell's been going on in here? Has there been any trouble, Iris?

Iris No, Cass, no trouble at all. We've just been keeping Jem amused.

Cass Yes, thank you for babysitting. I didn't honestly think I'd be gone quite so long—but I'm glad you managed to cope anyway...

Iris My pleasure, Cass. My pleasure entirely.

Cass (*going out; calling*) All right, come along then, son Jem, what about that tea…?

Cass goes out after Jem

The lights that have previously been off on the consoles are restored. All the panels are now glowing again

Iris (*calmly as ever*) Emergency now concluded. All systems normal…

The Lights slowly fade to Black-out

FURNITURE AND PROPERTY LIST

ACT I

On stage: Bank of control panels, computer consoles, and monitor screens
Sliding drawer. *In it:* monitors, life supports and dummy Elise
Control desk and chair mounted on a low revolving rostrum, which
    has a junction box with electrical wires inside
Toy gun
Tool cupboard. *In it:* unusual-looking technical equipment and
    tools, a robust inspection camera, vacuum welding gun, adhesive
    tape, spanner
Cupboard 10 (practical)

ACT II

On stage: As before

Off stage: Dried-up macaroni cheese on a plate (**Damaris**)
Tool case. *In it:* walkie-talkie radio (**Cass**)

Personal: **Cass:** helmet with darkened face plate

LIGHTING PLOT

Property fittings required: flickering control panel lights, glowing monitor screens, green/red airlock lights
Interior. The same scene throughout

ACT I

To open: Overall general lighting

Cue 1	**Jem** and **Damaris** go off *Dim main lights*	(Page 22)
Cue 2	**Iris**: "Are you there, Callisto Two?" *Flashing red light on the console*	(Page 22)
Cue 3	The alarm is set off again *Flashing red lights all over the control panel;* *then, swiftly fade to black-out*	(Page 25)

ACT II

To open: Overall general lighting

Cue 4	**Iris**: "I am now opening the internal airlock." *Flash lights around the main door*	(Page 29)
Cue 5	The door closes completely *Stop flashing lights around the main door*	(Page 29)
Cue 6	**Iris**: "I am opening the inner airlock door." *Flash lights around the main door*	(Page 35)
Cue 7	The door closes *Stop flashing lights around the main door*	(Page 36)
Cue 8	**Iris**: "I am now opening the inner airlock door." *Flash lights around the main door*	(Page 40)

| *Cue* 9 | The door closes | (Page 40) |
| | *Stop flashing lights around the main door* | |

| *Cue* 10 | **Jem** presses the trigger on the welder | (Page 47) |
| | *Flash of light from one of the cupboards* | |

| *Cue* 11 | **Jem** fires | (Page 47) |
| | *Flash of light* | |

| *Cue* 12 | **Jem** fires | (Page 48) |
| | *Flash of light* | |

| *Cue* 13 | **Jem** fires | (Page 48) |
| | *Flash of light* | |

| *Cue* 14 | The gun on the desk fires | (Page 49) |
| | *Flash of light inches from where* **Jem** *had been standing* | |

| *Cue* 15 | **Jem**: "Iris, you could be right…" | (Page 49) |
| | *Gun fires again* | |

| *Cue* 16 | The gun fires into cupboard 10 | (Page 50) |
| | *Flash of light from cupboard 10* | |

| *Cue* 17 | The gun fires into the tool cupboard | (Page 50) |
| | *Flash of light from the tool cupboard* | |

| *Cue* 18 | **Iris**: "The inner airlock door is now opening." | (Page 54) |
| | *Flash lights around the main door* | |

| *Cue* 19 | **Cass** goes out after **Jem** | (Page 57) |
| | *Snap on all lights on the consoles* | |

| *Cue* 20 | **Iris**: "All systems normal…" | (Page 57) |
| | *Slowly fade to black-out* | |

EFFECTS PLOT

ACT I

ACT II

Cue 11	The main door closes completely *Cut beeping*	(Page 29)
Cue 12	The picture on the monitor screens changes *Hissing sound over the microphone, and a differently pitched beeping sound*	(Page 29)
Cue 13	**Iris**: "Is everything satisfactory, Damaris?" **Damaris's Voice** *as script pages 30-35*	(Page 30)
Cue 14	**Iris**: "I am now closing the external airlock." *Further hissing sound; cut beeping sound when ready*	(Page 30)
Cue 15	**Jem** and **Iris** listen *Regular and quite rapid rasping sound*	(Page 31)
Cue 16	**Damaris** is silent *Louder strange breathing*	(Page 32)
Cue 17	**Jem**: "Why can't Damaris see it?" *Steadily increase volume of strange breathing to very loud*	(Page 33)
Cue 18	**Iris**: "I am now opening the external airlock door…" *Hissing sound as before, followed by the external warning beep*	(Page 34)
Cue 19	**Iris**: "I am now closing the external airlock door." *Further hissing sound as the door closes*	(Page 35)
Cue 20	The picture changes, to the external south-east view *Cut warning beeps as the external door closes*	(Page 35)
Cue 21	**Iris**: "I am opening the inner airlock door." *Hiss and beeps as the door opens*	(Page 35)
Cue 22	The door closes *Cut beeping when ready*	(Page 36)
Cue 23	**Iris**: "I am increasing my own input levels…" *Breathing sound fills the dome*	(Page 36)
Cue 24	**Damaris** begins to lurch forward after **Jem** *Increase breathing sound*	(Page 39)

Cue 25 **Iris**: "I am now opening the inner airlock door."   (Page 40)
Hissing and beeping sounds

Cue 26 The door closes   (Page 40)
Cut hissing and beeping sounds

Cue 27 **Iris**: "Listen for yourself."   (Page 41)
Damaris's Voice *as script pages 41-42*

Cue 28 **Damaris's Voice**: "Bye-bye."   (Page 42)
Beep from **Damaris**

Cue 29 **Jem**: "Where?"   (Page 43)
*Fade up breathing sounds and snarling noises as
    script pages 43-45*

Cue 30 **Jem** lays the camera down on the work top   (Page 45)
Rattling in cupboard 10

Cue 31 Cupboard 10 opens   (Page 47)
*Fade up breathing sounds and snarling noises as
    script pages 47-52*

Cue 32 **Jem** fires   (Page 47)
Puff of smoke

Cue 33 **Jem** fires   (Page 48)
Puff of smoke

Cue 34 **Jem** fires   (Page 48)
Puff of smoke

Cue 35 The gun on the desk fires   (Page 49)
Puff of smoke inches from where **Jem** *had been standing*

Cue 36 **Jem**: "Iris, you could be right…"   (Page 49)
Puff of smoke

Cue 37 The gun fires into cupboard 10   (Page 50)
Puff of smoke from cupboard 10

Cue 38 The gun fires into the tool cupboard   (Page 50)
Puff of smoke from the tool cupboard

Cue 39	**Jem** appears to touch **The Thing** with the wires *Fearful screeching sound, and smoke*	(Page 52)
Cue 40	**Iris**: "There was only a three point seven…" *Intruder alarm buzzes*	(Page 53)
Cue 41	**Jem**: "Well, tell it to tidy up, OK?" *Hissing and beeping sounds*	(Page 53)
Cue 42	**Iris**: "The airlock is now repressurizing." *Hissing sound from the airlock*	(Page 53)
Cue 43	**Iris**: "The inner airlock door is now opening." *Beeping of the main door*	(Page 54)
Cue 44	**Cass**: "C Five to Beta." **Keren's Voice** *as script page 56*	(Page 56)

PRINTED IN GREAT BRITAIN BY
THE LONGDUNN PRESS LTD., BRISTOL.